OTABENGA

John Strand

BROADWAY PLAY PUBLISHING INC
224 E 62nd St, NY, NY 10065
www.broadwayplaypub.com
info@broadwayplaypub.com

OTABENGA
© Copyright 2008 by John Strand

First printing: December 2008
I S B N: 0-88145-403-6

Book design: Marie Donovan
Word processing: Microsoft Word
Typographic controls: Ventura Publisher
Typeface: Palatino
Printed and bound in the U S A

ABOUT THE AUTHOR

John Strand is a winner and three-time nominee of the Charles MacArthur Award for Playwriting. His most recent work includes the book and lyrics for AN ITALIAN STRAW HAT: A VAUDEVILLE, a new musical with a score by composer Dennis McCarthy, premiering at South Coast Repertory, Costa Mesa, Calif.; LINCOLNESQUE, a dark comedy about politics and madness in Washington, DC, (The Cleveland Play House, directed by Michael Bloom); and LORENZACCIO, his adaptation of Alfred de Musset's 1834 French classic (The Shakespeare Theater, Washington, DC, directed by Michael Kahn). Strand is the author of the book for the musical THE HIGHEST YELLOW, with a score by Michael John LaChiusa, at Signature Theater, Arlington, Va. His other plays include Lovers and Executioners, Arena Stage, winner of the Charles MacArthur Award for Outstanding New Play; THE DIARIES, commissioned by Signature Theater and nominated for the MacArthur; TOM WALKER, commissioned by Arena Stage. Additional plays are THE MISER, an adaptation of the Molière play set in Reagan-era America, at Arena Stage; THREE NIGHTS IN TEHRAN, a comedy about the Iran-Contra affair, Signature Theater; THE COCKBURN RITUALS, Woolly Mammoth Theater. Strand spent ten years in Paris, where he worked as a journalist and drama critic, writing in English and French, and directed New York University's Experimental Theater Wing in Paris.

OTABENGA premiered at Signature Theater,
Arlington, Va., on 19 November 1994, directed by
Michael Kahn. The cast and creative contributors were:

OTABENGA .... Ramon Melindez Moses
VERNER .... Wallace Acton
W J CHIEF MCGEE .... Buzz Mauro
MISS FAIRCHILD .... Deb Gottesman
MASISI, REVEREND GORDON .... Doug Brown
BAMBUTI WOMAN, INSTRUCTRESS .... Tia Howell
WILLIAM TEMPLE HORNADAY .... Bill Delaney
MADISON GRANT .... Grover Gardner

Director .... Michael Kahn
Set design .... Tony Cisek
Lights .... John Burchett
Costumes .... Cathy Christovitch
Choreography .... Karen A Daniels
Sound .... David Maddox.

The playwright gratefully acknowledges the support of the following individuals and organizations:

The development of this play was made possible by Signature Theater of Arlington, Va., Eric D Schaeffer, Artistic director, through its "Stages" Series, Marcia Gardner, director.

Further assistance was provided by the Shenandoah Playwrights Retreat, a project of ShenanArts; and by the John F Kennedy Center for the Performing Arts, through its Jack Morrison Fellowship in playwriting.

Thanks to the staff of the South Caroliniana Library, University of South Carolina, Columbia, SC, for their research assistance; and to the Missouri Historical Society, Saint Louis.

Very special thanks to Roland L Reed and to Eric D Schaeffer for their encouragement and expertise throughout the development of this play.

INTRODUCTION

In 1904 the city of Saint Louis hosted a world's fair, officially titled the Louisiana Purchase Exposition, commemorating America's purchase of a vast chunk of its Midwest territory from Napoleon one hundred years before. The Saint Louis Fair, like ones before it, was meant to be the greatest and most spectacular the world had ever seen.

One of its events was titled the "University of Man". To celebrate the emerging science of anthropology, "race specimens" from around the world were gathered and brought to Saint Louis to be displayed for the crowds: Indians, Eskimos, Africans and other "rare" races. The explicit purpose was to measure scientifically the capabilities of these so-called primitive cultures according to popular notions of biological evolution.

A young southerner and self-styled African explorer, Samuel Phillips Verner, made three trips to the Belgian Congo during this period. Two of these trips were as a Special Agent for the Saint Louis Fair. Verner brought back with him several pygmies, one of whom was Otabenga.

The play recounts how Otabenga was purchased by Verner from another African tribe and persuaded to come to America; how he was displayed as a race specimen at the Saint Louis Fair; how he later accompanied a financially destitute Verner to New York where he was sold to the Bronx Zoo and displayed there, for a time in a cage with a chimpanzee; how he was released after public protests; and how he remained in America, making an ultimately vain attempt to adapt to American life.

Otabenga committed suicide in Lynchburg, Virginia, in 1916.

In the play, historical figures are present, if in invented form: W J "Chief" McGee, a leading American anthropologist and official of the Saint Louis Fair; William Temple Hornaday, head of the New York Zoological Society; Madison Grant, his colleague and an essayist on the superiority of the Aryan race; Reverend James H Gordon, leader of the Colored Baptist Ministers Conference. In some cases, I have borrowed and reworked points of view they left behind in published works of the period. But the play is based on historical events at the turn of the 20th century, as documented in newspaper accounts and various publications of the period, as well as in letters, personal papers and unpublished manuscripts.

The heart of the play, though, remains the relationship between Verner and Otabenga, what each man meant to the other, and what each learned from the other. The story follows their personal journeys through America at the turn of the 20th century, a society perhaps at the height of its promise, its self-confidence, and its arrogance.

CAST

The play calls for 8 actors: 2 women, 6 men. Of these, 3 are black (one woman, two men) and 5 white (one woman, four men).

The actors play a total of 29 roles. These are, in order of stage appearance:

SAMUEL PHILLIPS VERNER, *explorer, late twenties*
OTABENGA, *Bambuti (pygmy), mid-twenties*
NURSE
BOARDMEMBER 1 *of the Stillman Institute, Tuscaloosa, Ala.*
BOARDMEMBER 2
BOARDMEMBER 3
Ship's OFFICER
W J "Chief" MCGEE, *head of Anthropology for the Saint Louis World's Fair of 1904*
MISS FAIRCHILD, *assistant to* MCGEE
MASISI, *Bambuti male, thirties*
MASAMBA, *Bambuti female, twenties*
A Belgian SOLDIER
REPORTER
TUBA PLAYER
FAIRGOER 1
FAIRGOER 2
FLOOR WALKER
BAMBUTI WOMAN
A railway PORTER
A railway CHIEF PORTER
A railway PASSENGER
WILLIAM TEMPLE HORNADAY, *Director of the Bronx Zoo*

MADISON GRANT, *Zoo Treasurer and racial theorist*
REVEREND JAMES H GORDON, *a spiritual leader of New York's black community*
CITIZEN 1
CITIZEN 2
CITIZEN 3
INTRUCTRESS, *Howard Colored Orphans Asylum*
MANAGER

SETTING

The action of the play takes place in the United States and Africa from 1896 to 1916.

A NOTE

It is important that the actors portraying the Africans avoid any clichéd "primitive" or foreign dialect. When they speak among themselves, they should do so naturally with no unusual accent. When the character VERNER is outside his own culture and speaks haltingly in a foreign language, he too should avoid a false accent.

The actor playing OTABENGA should not be small of stature. An average-sized actor in this role reinforces the impression that Westerners at the turn of the 20th century, despite their society's professed admiration for the empirical method, sometimes allowed their preconceptions to obscure the facts of what they observed.

for Amanda

Ex Africa semper aliquid novi.
—Pliny the Elder

(Something unexpected always comes from Africa)

Prologue

(1916. A sanitarium in Baltimore, although we are not sure of that just yet. Downstage, in a narrow strip of light, a man wearing a wrinkled and stained white cotton suit, Panama hat. Behind him, in shadow, a metal-frame hospital bed. Further upstage, in deeper shadow barely visible, sit two men and a woman)

VERNER: The hunt! That's what I remember best, the hunt. The deep shadow of the jungle forest broken by diamonds of light that fall through the roof of leaves above, like the light from the windows of a great cathedral. We crouch and wait. We hear only our hearts, eager to kill. The signal! We rise and begin to run, shouting out the hunting cry— "Takaa, takaa!" —sprinting through the dark green mist, driving the game toward the nets. There's one! Okapi. A great prize. He flashes in one direction, changes course, then leaps as though he can fly. "There's a spirit in him!" someone cries, and we, too, flash and leap, inspired by the animal's power and grace. Then suddenly, he's caught! The surprise in his wild eyes as we leap on him and plunge our knives through the beautiful velvet coat, the hot blood on our arms and chests, the triumph in our wild eyes, the victim's final shudder, his sigh of acceptance, and it's over. *(A beat)* Actually? I made that up. They never let me go on the hunt. But it doesn't matter. I'm inventing my own Africa now.

(A beat. Enter OTABENGA. *He is dressed identically to* VERNER*)*

VERNER: "Empire Building in Central Africa: True Tales of Exploration by Professor Reverend Doctor Samuel P Verner, the Man Who Brought The Pygmies To America." I have been unable to interest a publisher. Publishers are idiots. I opened up the African continent. People knew me. I was in the newspapers. I lived with the pygmies! *(He makes a scary face on the word.)* They worshipped me.

OTABENGA: *(Calmly)* They would have cut your throat.

VERNER: *(Undeterred)* One of them came back to America with me. I trained him in religion, taught him some English. I tried to help him, but he would not fit in.

OTABENGA: He was locked in a cage, displayed like a beast.

VERNER: He insists on haunting me. Invading my memory.

OTABENGA: Memory is a slippery place. You need some help.

VERNER: I have endured a great deal. My condition is grave. I could die.

OTABENGA: You're already dead.

VERNER: Leave me alone!

(One of the upstage figures, a NURSE, approaches. She cannot see OTABENGA. She hands VERNER a metal basin)

NURSE: Specimen, Reverend.

(She waits as VERNER turns his back, prepares to urinate)

OTABENGA: Consider how alike we are, Fwela.

VERNER: I will not!

NURSE: You will so.

VERNER: I am a scientist!

NURSE: Scientists pee, too. Any visits from the Pygmy today?

OTABENGA: Yes.

VERNER: No! I need my privacy.

NURSE: Regulations.

(VERNER *hurls the basin to the floor.*)

VERNER: I can't! Have someone bring my things. I am leaving.

NURSE: Not today, Reverend. (*She returns to her place and sits.*)

VERNER: I wish I'd never met you.

OTABENGA: You loved me, Fwela.

VERNER: "Love"? "Felt affection," maybe.

OTABENGA: Loved me. Your finest moment.

VERNER: What good did it do me? You ruined me. And yourself. (*Angrily*) You're not even here!

(*They both sit on the bed.*)

OTABENGA: (*The figures in shadow*) They're watching you.

VERNER: They insist on "helping me". I'm scared.

OTABENGA: They can't take it away, Fwela.

VERNER: They might.

OTABENGA: Tell them.

VERNER: It's all I have left.

OTABENGA: Yours, forever.

VERNER: My Africa.

(*The sound of church bells.* VERNER *stands, comes downstage*)

VERNER: I was young, full of dreams. I graduate at the top of my class at the seminary. "Please, Verner," they beg me. "Go to Africa. Bring the word of God to the natives!" And there began all my troubles.

(OTABENGA *exits.*)

END OF PROLOGUE

ACT ONE

Scene One

(Three figures approach: they are BOARDMEMBERS *of the Stillman Institute, Alabama. It is 1894. The* BOARDMEMBERS *are being very hard on* VERNER, *age twenty, as they question his plan, his motives, his sanity)*

BOARDMEMBER 1: Africa, Verner?

VERNER: Sir, yes! Africa.

BOARDMEMBER 2: Ridiculous.

BOARDMEMBER 3: He's been reading Livingstone.

BOARDMEMBER 2: You are not Doctor Livingstone, I presume?

BOARDMEMBER 1: The Stillman Institute did not establish our mission in the Congo so young men could go play hero.

BOARDMEMBER 2: You don't know the first thing about Africa.

VERNER: God, science and commerce.

BOARDMEMBER 3: "Science"?

VERNER: The three weapons for a conquest of Africa.

BOARDMEMBER 2: It is not a war.

VERNER: Oh but it is, sir! For the soul of Africa. And we, the Caucasian race, being the most highly evolved—

BOARDMEMBER 3: He's been reading Darwin!

VERNER: It is our duty as Christians to rescue the Africans, the least evolved, before they fall prey to the Asians, the Asians being, sir, about mid-way evolved, probably.

(A beat)

BOARDMEMBER 1: He's got a point.

VERNER: Let me go, sirs!

BOARDMEMBER 1: You, Verner? Or the Emperor of Austria?

VERNER: I am better now.

BOARDMEMBER 3: Committed to a sanitarium.

VERNER: Nervous exhaustion—

BOARDMEMBER 2: Confess the real reason you want to go.

BOARDMEMBER 3: You covet wealth!

VERNER: Every dollar of mine will be a dollar for God.

BOARDMEMBER 2: Not sufficient.

VERNER: And for the Stillman Institute.

BOARDMEMBER 3: That's somewhat better.

BOARDMEMBER 1: All missionaries are strictly required to pass a three-year program of study. You've been here three weeks.

VERNER: Four weeks, sir.

BOARDMEMBER 2: We do have standards.

VERNER: You have Negroes, sir. Running your mission in Africa. Being paid the same rate as white men. God forbid the newspapers get a hold of it.

BOARDMEMBER 1: Are you trying to pressure us, Verner?

VERNER: With all respect, sir: yes. The fact is, you can't find a single white man willing to risk his life in the Congo. Except me.

(A beat)

BOARDMEMBER 2: Have you seen the casualty figures, Verner?

VERNER: Of the natives, sir?

BOARDMEMBER 2: The missionaries.

VERNER: Why, no, I—

BOARDMEMBER 1: "Reverend" Verner.

(A BOARDMEMBER tosses a pith helmet to VERNER)

VERNER: Almost immediately, I think—

BOARDMEMBER 1: When can you get started?

(A suitcase is tossed to him)

BOARDMEMBER 1: Write to us. Oh, and Verner: the emphasis is God. Science and commerce can wait. We've got to convert the savages before we can turn them into scholars and capitalists.

VERNER: Yes, sir! And thank you, sir! You won't regret this!

BOARDMEMBER 1: I hope you can say the same one day, Samuel.

(Sounds of a ship's whistle. Stirring Sousa-style music of the period as two of the BOARDMEMBERS withdraw. A third, however, places a naval officer's hat on his head and becomes a SHIP'S OFFICER. He hangs a circular life saver on the iron rail of the bed. He and VERNER are now onboard a transatlantic steamer as it approaches the coast of Africa)

Scene Two

(At sea, nearing the coast of Africa)

VERNER: Africa! Where evolution began—but somehow got bogged down.

SHIP'S OFFICER: You're a scientist?

VERNER: To the depths of my soul, sir!

SHIP'S OFFICER: I thought you were a missionary.

VERNER: My mission is science, commerce, and God.

SHIP'S OFFICER: Should be room for all three. It's a big country.

VERNER: Eleven million square miles. Chiefly rubber, copper, ivory, and precious minerals. Virtually no cotton.

SHIP'S OFFICER: A man could make a fortune.

VERNER: Human labor: that's the key.

SHIP'S OFFICER: All those natives.

VERNER: Unemployed.

SHIP'S OFFICER: You've been to Africa?

VERNER: Oh, several times. Mostly along the coast, there.

SHIP'S OFFICER: All the action's in the interior.

VERNER: The Congo.

SHIP'S OFFICER: Loads of slaughtering in the Congo.

VERNER: Slaughtering?

SHIP'S OFFICER: Oh, rivers of blood. Belgians murdering all the natives.

VERNER: But that's impossible.

SHIP'S OFFICER: Africa's a great continent for impossibles.

VERNER: The Treaty of Berlin, 1884— The slave trade has been banned.

SHIP'S OFFICER: Slave labor's the game now. They give the natives quotas. If they don't meet their quotas— *(He makes a gesture)* A man I know says the corpses are piled higher than the rubber trees. *(A beat)* You look a little green, Reverend. Good luck with that fortune of yours.

(The ship's whistle blows. Lights change; music. The SHIP'S OFFICER *swings the bed around one full turn. Return voyage:* VERNER *now appears broken, ill)*

SHIP'S OFFICER: Two years on the dark continent? How would you describe life in the interior, Reverend?

VERNER: Carnage.

SHIP'S OFFICER: Bring God to the natives, did you?

VERNER: They have their own gods.

SHIP'S OFFICER: Ever get that business scheme off the ground? Cotton, wasn't it? *(Coughing sounds from* VERNER*)* Where are you returning to? New York?

VERNER: My empire. Austria.

SHIP'S OFFICER: Say, Reverend: looks like you brought back a little brain fever.

VERNER: Feeling top-notch.

*(*VERNER *nearly collapses. Music.* SHIP'S OFFICER *strolls off, with bed. Enter* MCGEE *and* MISS FAIRCHILD. MCGEE *wheels a table-top scale model of the Saint Louis World's Fair; she wheels a wooden office chair. She deftly scoops up* VERNER *and wheels him into position for the next scene.)*

Scene Three

(The office of W J "Chief" McGee, head of Anthropology for the Louisiana Purchase Exposition of 1904, popularly known as the Saint Louis World's Fair)

MCGEE: Picture dirigibles.

MISS FAIRCHILD: A half dozen or more.

MCGEE: Blotting out the sun.

MISS FAIRCHILD: The moon.

MCGEE: Hovering like giant, silent honeybees. Inside them: telegraph experts in constant touch with Chicago, Illinois.

MISS FAIRCHILD: The world shrinks.

MCGEE: I give you the choice of any man on earth to run telegraphic communications for the Saint Louis World's Fair of 1904. Who do you take?

VERNER: I— I'd have to think—

MCGEE: Guglielmo Marconi.

MISS FAIRCHILD: We wanted him, they gave him to us.

MCGEE: Alexander Graham Bell.

MISS FAIRCHILD: Max Weber.

MCGEE: Helen Keller on hand to welcome the blind customers. This thing is so big, Reverend—

MISS FAIRCHILD: So enormous—

MCGEE: You can't even begin to imagine it. I've been here three years, I still haven't grasped it. I brought Miss Fairchild on, what? A year ago?

MISS FAIRCHILD: Year and a half.

MCGEE: You don't usually see a woman this high up. She's a tough little nut, Reverend. Don't underestimate her.

VERNER: I won't.

MCGEE: In four months, we open a world's fair. We change history.

MISS FAIRCHILD: One thousand, three hundred acres.

MCGEE: You can't see it in a day.

MISS FAIRCHILD: You can't see it in a month.

MCGEE: The Saint Louis Pike: one linear mile of the best the 20th century has to offer. Visit the moon.

MISS FAIRCHILD: Visit Dante's Paradise.

MCGEE: Sip German beer in a German beer garden.

MISS FAIRCHILD: Revisit the Johnstown Flood.

MCGEE: Relive the Boer War. On opening night, President Theodore Roosevelt, a thousand miles away in Washington, DC, hits a switch, and bingo.

MISS FAIRCHILD: The 20th century begins in earnest.

MCGEE: One million electric lights. You're a seasoned traveler, Reverend. You may have seen a full-grown elephant slide down a chute into a pool of water— but at night?

(A beat. They stare at VERNER, awaiting a reply.)

VERNER: I hardly know what to say.

MCGEE: I'm a scientist, Reverend. And a businessman. The science of this business boils down to one thing.

MISS FAIRCHILD: Entertainment.

MCGEE: That's where the pygmies come in.

VERNER: The pygmies?

MCGEE: Why do you want to come work for the Saint Louis World's Fair, Reverend?

VERNER: The whole project— Inspiring. And then, my personal finances are presently...

MISS FAIRCHILD: You're broke.

MCGEE: Did a little research on you, Reverend. Impressive credentials. Two years in the bush. Ever get that cotton scheme off the ground?

VERNER: Hard to do business in that heat.

MISS FAIRCHILD: Any conversions?

VERNER: Of currency?

MISS FAIRCHILD: Of the natives.

VERNER: Oh. Yes, ma'am. The Congo is crawling with Christians now.

MCGEE: How's your health?

VERNER: *My* health? Top notch.

MISS FAIRCHILD: Enjoy your stay in the sanitarium?

VERNER: Slight touch of malaria.

MCGEE: May I be frank, Reverend? A World's Fair cannot afford to associate with anyone in less than top-notch mental health. So let's not mention the incident again.

MISS FAIRCHILD: Especially to the press.

MCGEE: You speak the language, Reverend?

VERNER: Fluently. Which language?

MCGEE: Pygmy.

VERNER: Like a native.

MCGEE: "University of Man." That's the concept. All the important lower races: Apaches, Eskimos,

Zulus, Giant Patagonians and hairy Ainus. On view live in faithful reproductions of their native habitats.

MISS FAIRCHILD: Thoroughly scientific.

MCGEE: A walk back through the evolutionary process, top to bottom.

MISS FAIRCHILD: How far have they been left behind?

MCGEE: And what can the Caucasian race do to help?

MISS FAIRCHILD: If anything.

(A beat, and a sigh from MCGEE)

MCGEE: We have to try.

MISS FAIRCHILD: We can't teach them to evolve.

MCGEE: We can study the phenomenon. Science has worked wonders.

MISS FAIRCHILD: But not miracles.

MCGEE: We unlocked the secret of the telephone.

MISS FAIRCHILD: What would a Patagonian do with a telephone?

MCGEE: That's what we need to study.

MISS FAIRCHILD: Ridiculous.

MCGEE: Miss Fairchild is a Repatriationist, Reverend. Send the Negro back to Africa.

MISS FAIRCHILD: I have a right to my opinion.

MCGEE: Even when it's wrong. What's your stance on Repatriation, Reverend?

VERNER: Well, Chief McGee, personally I— What's your opinion?

MCGEE: An abomination.

VERNER: My thoughts exactly.

MCGEE: The gift of civilization. That's what we must offer them, right here in our own country.

MISS FAIRCHILD: False promises, shattered dreams.

MCGEE: Miss Fairchild is also a polygenist. You're not a polygenist, Reverend, I hope?

VERNER: Me, sir?

MISS FAIRCHILD: God created two Adams. One white, one black. It's that simple.

MCGEE: What about the yellow race?

MISS FAIRCHILD: So there were three Adams.

MCGEE: The brown race?

MISS FAIRCHILD: Or four.

MCGEE: The red race?

MISS FAIRCHILD: Or five or six, what difference does it make!?

MCGEE: *(To* VERNER*)* You see what I have to put up with?

MISS FAIRCHILD: The way to help is to restore their dignity—

MCGEE: We have a duty—

(Simultaneously)

MISS FAIRCHILD: —by sending them back!

MCGEE: —to help them!

MCGEE: *(Restraining his temper)* This Fair is about harmony and evolution. And if we have not evolved to where I can demand harmony and get it, then there will be some changes in this office.

*(*MISS FAIRCHILD *sulks.)*

MCGEE: Reverend: I name you a Special Agent of the Saint Louis Fair. Go back to Africa. Return with one dozen pygmies. I'll take four adult hunters, four adult females, none pregnant, two children, preferably male, a medicine man and one elder chieftain in full dress. Any questions?

VERNER: What if they don't want to come?

MCGEE: To the event of the century? Have you thought about a budget?

VERNER: No. I mean, ten thousand ought to cover it.

MCGEE: Do you have any idea what your personal gain is likely to be? Special Agent Reverend Doctor Verner: The Man Who Brought Back the Pygmies. I can offer you five hundred dollars. When can you leave?

VERNER: Almost immediately, I think.

MCGEE: Write to us. A new century, Reverend, is being launched right here. World peace, prosperity, universal understanding await us. Good hunting!

(Snappy military music. MCGEE and MISS FAIRCHILD withdraw, with chair and model. Silence. First sounds of the forest. VERNER grips his suitcase, glances nervously around, collapses.)

END OF ACT ONE

ACT TWO

Scene One

(The Belgian Congo. An encampment at dusk. Two of the Bambuti people, OTABENGA *and* MASISI, *stand over* VERNER's *prone body, observing him. His open suitcase lies beside him.* OTABENGA *wears a light cotton suit-coat, evidently one that belongs to* VERNER. *A beat)*

MASISI: Look at this shit. Can you believe this? It's disgraceful. Why do they come here? That's my question. They show up, make noise, get sick and collapse.

OTABENGA: They do it to help us.

(A look from MASISI)

OTABENGA: Well, that's what they say.

MASISI: Completely white. Nothing that ugly could be anything but trouble.

OTABENGA: Manilabo says they're from the Land of the Dead. They shed their skin.

MASISI: That's why they wear all these clothes. To hide it. They're cannibals, you know.

OTABENGA: They are not.

(MASISI rummages through VERNER's *suitcase, takes a can of food, a commercial brand with a picture of a child on it)*

MASISI: Look at this. Right on the can. They don't even try to hide it.

OTABENGA: He didn't eat me.

MASISI: He bought you. Now he owns you.

OTABENGA: He didn't "buy" me. He paid for me to go free.

MASISI: "Free"? Don't be a fool. The Land of the Dead?

OTABENGA: What would it be like to hunt there?

MASISI: Otabenga!

OTABENGA: There must be more than one way to enter.

MASISI: The way your wife and child did. And the *muzungu* sent them there.

OTABENGA: Belgians killed my family. This one's not a Belgian.

MASISI: A *muzungu* is a *muzungu*.

OTABENGA: What are they, really? Aren't you curious?

MASISI: Imagine their women! Oh!

OTABENGA: He comes here, completely alone. That's either very brave, or very stupid.

MASISI: It's very stupid. *(Finding something in the suitcase)* Look: cigarettes.

(MASISI *takes some cigarettes for himself)*

OTABENGA: If you could just understand them, there would be nothing left to fear.

MASISI: Like your animals. Everything to you is the hunt.

OTABENGA: That's what I do best.

(OTABENGA *gestures.* MASISI *gives him a few cigarettes)*

MASISI: Now death is hunting you, Otabenga. That's what everyone says. Your family, slaughtered. Now you bring this here.

(VERNER *stirs, then sits up suddenly, as if in alarm. He appears feverish and frightened. He rummages in his pocket for a tiny, dog-eared booklet, which he frantically consults.*)

VERNER: Ditchwater! Lion dung at evening!

(*A beat.* OTABENGA *and* MASISI *look at one another.*)

MASISI: I don't believe it. He's trying to speak the language.

VERNER: Ditchwater. Eat my campfire.

MASISI: Listen to that accent!

VERNER: I am your bowl. Circumsize me...!

(VERNER *collapses into a state of semi-consciousness.* OTABENGA *kneels beside him, cradles his head in his hands.*)

OTABENGA: It's a fever. He's burning up. Go and bring Masamba.

MASISI: What for?

OTABENGA: He may die.

MASISI: He's already dead.

OTABENGA: Masisi.

(*Exit* MASISI)

OTABENGA: How many times can the dead die? (*A beat*) Now it's my turn to save you. Then we'll be equal.

(*African music. The two men stand and face the audience. A beat. At the same instant, they begin to play the next scene.*)

Scene Two

(A forest clearing. Day. Sounds of the forest. OTABENGA *instructing* VERNER. OTABENGA, *wearing two or three cigarettes behind his ears, crouches,* VERNER *attempts to do the same. Beginning here and increasingly throughout the following scenes,* OTABENGA *will wear more elements of* VERNER's *clothing.* VERNER, *consequently, will wear and possess less)*

OTABENGA: *(Pointing)* "Bird."

VERNER: "Bard."

OTABENGA: "Bird."

VERNER: "Bird."

OTABENGA: Good. You're getting stronger every day. We almost lost you, you know. This, where we are now: "forest".

VERNER: "Farest."

OTABENGA: Behind us, where we crossed: "river". Two days down river is the village. Villagers are prisoners of their houses. But we're free. We move with the hunt.

VERNER: Hunt! Verner!

OTABENGA: I can't teach you that. The hunt is within you, or it's not. You have to become your prey, until your true self is invisible to him. But my friend: you're too ugly to hunt.

VERNER: "Ugly."

OTABENGA: *(Laughing at him)* And loud. And clumsy. You can't even pee without knocking over a tree.

VERNER: "Ugly"!

OTABENGA: But I like you. We'll call you *"Fwela"*: "leader". You who are alone. *"Fwela."*

VERNER: *"Fwela."*

OTABENGA: It's a joke. Do you get it?

VERNER: *"Fwela"*!

OTABENGA: Sometimes, *Fwela,* the hunt takes you far away. You follow, and discover things you never dreamed of. *(He takes a talisman that he is wearing around his neck.)* Here. *(He slips it over VERNER's head.)* Good fortune. In whatever you hunt.

VERNER: Me for?

OTABENGA: For you.

(Music. Same transition as last scene: they stare at the audience, then go into the next scene at the same moment.)

Scene Three

(OTABENGA and VERNER. Another clearing, another day. VERNER's education continues.)

OTABENGA: Remember what I told you yesterday about trees. Show me the mongongo tree.

(VERNER points, OTABENGA shakes his head. OTABENGA kneels, VERNER joins him)

OTABENGA: You're a slow learner. Look here. The forest has everything you need. This you can eat. This you cannot.

(A Bambuti woman, MASAMBA, crosses. VERNER stands, stares. OTABENGA pulls him back down.)

OTABENGA: That can eat you. *(A beat)* There's nothing to fear within the forest. All bad comes from outside. My people came from the forest, long before the rivers of now were rivers at all. And the forest takes us back when our lives are done. There is a belief: the greatest hunters become forest spirits, and live forever in every leaf, every root. *(A beat)* The others are watching you. Do you see them? Behind the trees. They wonder what kind of ghost you are.

VERNER: Can eat?

OTABENGA: Yes, you can eat that. They don't trust me, either. I spend too much time talking to ghosts. How well have you learned to see, Fwela? *(Pointing)* Over there: mongongo.

VERNER: "Mongongo."

OTABENGA: Look up... There. Do you see? Panther.

(OTABENGA exits silently. VERNER stares, trying to see.)

VERNER: "Pan-ther"... *(A beat. Seeing it)* Oh shit!

(Lights fade to low. Music. Same transition as last scene)

Scene Four

(VERNER in the encampment, composing a letter. Opposite, upstage, MCGEE and MISS FAIRCHILD, in their Saint Louis office)

VERNER: "...the pleasure to inform you that at last, despite constant danger to my life, I have located the pygmies. I am treated as a king among them. They refer to me as "Fwela", Bambuti for 'leader'."

(MCGEE and MISS FAIRCHILD respond to the news.)

MCGEE: He's found them! Take a press release: "Reverend Special Agent Verner, battling death and disease, tiny cannibal savages, etc."

VERNER: "You will be pleased to know that I am taking copious scientific notes. Why did the pygmy fail to evolve?..."

MCGEE: "Copious notes"? In two months, I am opening a world's fair. Tell him to load those pygmies on a boat and get back here pronto.

VERNER: "Given my success in the bush, I expect you to employ me, upon my return, in the Anthropology Department. Fifty dollars a week would satisfy me. Cable your acceptance of this proposal."

MCGEE: He's trying to blackmail me.

MISS FAIRCHILD: I warned you about him.

MCGEE: I requested a dozen pygmies. I do not need a reverend anthropologist.

MISS FAIRCHILD: Is he a reverend? What proof do we have?

VERNER: "My expenses are mounting. Cable another five hundred dollars immediately and have the money brought to Luebo."

(*Unseen by* VERNER, OTABENGA *has entered and stands a short distance behind him. He is observing* VERNER. *He mimics* VERNER's *physical movements, subtly at first, then with more confidence*)

MCGEE: Take a cable. "My Dear Verner: Congratulations, etc. But the Negroes are useless to us there. It is imperative, Reverend, nay crucial, that you bring home the pygmies now."

MISS FAIRCHILD: I don't like the "nay crucial".

MCGEE: What's wrong with it?

MISS FAIRCHILD: Too pleading. Too indecisive.

MCGEE: No it isn't.

MISS FAIRCHILD: Threaten him.

VERNER: "One of the pygmies is the cleverest little fellow. I purchased him from a neighboring tribe that had taken him prisoner. He cost me one pound of salt and a bolt of cloth. He is now entirely devoted to me."

MCGEE: "If you fail to arrive on schedule with the natives...I could impose a lateness penalty of, say, five percent of your fee."

MISS FAIRCHILD: Weak, weak, weak.

MCGEE: I don't want to antagonize him.

MISS FAIRCHILD: Weak, weak, weak.

MCGEE: I need those pygmies!

(Lights down on MCGEE *and* MISS FAIRCHILD *as they exit)*

VERNER: "His name is Otabenga. His teeth are filed into sharp points, apparently a primitive custom. I plan to instruct him in the rudiments of the English language and Christian theology. He will make an excellent specimen." *(*VERNER *becomes aware that* OTABENGA *is behind him)* Fwela give big gift. Otabenga home. America.

OTABENGA: You'll take me back to the Land of the Dead?

VERNER: "Back." "Dead."

(They both smile and chuckle. Same transition as last scene)

Scene Five

(The forest, a few days later. VERNER, *trying to tell a story to* OTABENGA *and* MASISI. VERNER *is drawing in the dirt.)*

OTABENGA: Your god had a son who came from the sky?

VERNER: "Jesus."

MASISI: And he did magic for the people?

VERNER: And— And— *(He makes a motion of bowing and praying.)*

OTABENGA: You worship him.

VERNER: Otabenga.

OTABENGA: I should worship him? Why?

*(*VERNER *points to one of his drawings in the dirt.)*

OTABENGA: Because he died?

MASISI: Obviously a weak god. How did he die?

VERNER: Kill.

OTABENGA: Who killed him?

VERNER: We. I.

MASISI: *(To* OTABENGA*)* He's more dangerous than we think.

VERNER: For. Die for.

OTABENGA: He died for me? What good is that?

VERNER: Gift! Big.

OTABENGA: In the Land of the Dead, dying is highly valued.

MASISI: They're obsessed with death.

VERNER: Three! Three! *(He mimes death and resurrection.)*

OTABENGA: After three days. He came back from the dead?

MASISI: And then he was white like you. *(To OTABENGA)* You see? I told you. *(To VERNER)* And where is he now, this god?

(VERNER points to the sky.)

MASISI: You know, for a cannibal who barely knows how to talk, you're not a bad storyteller. But if no one believes you, what's the point?

(Exit MASISI and OTABENGA.)

VERNER: I better not tell them about eating the body and drinking the blood.

(Same transition as last scene)

Scene Six

(VERNER, composing a letter)

VERNER: "I am daily gaining insight into the savage mind. The pygmies have one ceremony, or game: they attack each other's grass huts with sticks, virtually destroying them, while the whole tribe roars with laughter. Then they spend days rebuilding the huts. At first, this struck me as foolishly destructive. But upon reflection, I find it...freeing. And it seems to satisfy them deeply.

"Did you know that the ancient Egyptians called the pygmies 'Dancers of God'?

"Three days ago, we entered a village, hoping to trade some meat. But the place was deserted, the wooden huts burnt. We found three bodies. The Batwa say that Belgian soldiers did it. But of course there is no proof. I suspect it was other Negroes..."

(MASAMBA, *running franticly, crosses. A beat and enter a Belgian* SOLDIER, *armed, in pursuit. He is unshaven, filthy. He stops when he encounters* VERNER... *He grabs the papers from* VERNER's *hand, glances at them, tosses them to the ground.*)

VERNER: Excuse me...? What do you think you're doing? I am an agent of the Saint Louis World's Fair.

(*The* SOLDIER *grabs* VERNER *by the throat. Terrified*)

VERNER: I am an ordained minister...!

(*The* SOLDIER *points his rifle at* VERNER's *head. On his knees, begging*)

VERNER: Don't shoot me! Please...

(*The* SOLDIER *kicks* VERNER *to the ground and exits.* VERNER *rises. Frightened, he calls out.*)

VERNER: Otabenga!

(*Lights fade to low. Chanting voices, fast, and frantic. Same transition as last scene*)

Scene Seven

(*A forest clearing, day.* VERNER, *with* OTABENGA *as his interpreter, addresses* MASISI)

VERNER: You. Fwela home you.

MASISI: The man has no facility with language.

OTABENGA: He wants you to return to his land with him.

VERNER: You. You. And you, you, you, you, you.

MASISI: He can't count either.

OTABENGA: He wants twelve of us to come to a great celebration. The *muzungu* will come from all their surrounding villages to see us.

MASISI: Why?

OTABENGA: It is a *muzungu* custom.

VERNER: You. Fwela home.

MASISI: I'll get to the Land of the Dead when my time comes, like everyone else.

OTABENGA: Fwela's kings have commanded him to invite us. It's my duty to help him.

MASISI: Help him go back to his own land where he belongs, before he does any more harm. What has he ever given us?

OTABENGA: Cigarettes.

MASISI: I don't care a damn for his cigarettes! What white man has ever brought anything but trouble?

OTABENGA: I choose to go with him.

MASISI: Go, then!

OTABENGA: You can stay here and get killed off by the Belgians.

MASISI: We'll go deeper into the forest.

OTABENGA: They'll find you wherever you go!

MASISI: Death is hunting you, Otabenga—and now he's got you. And he'll turn you white. *(He begins to exit, returns.)* Give me two cigarettes.

(OTABENGA does so. Exit MASISI.)

VERNER: *(Calling after him)* Fwela home! Home, home, home, godammit!!

(VERNER exits. OTABENGA sits and waits. Forest sounds, male voices chanting as night falls)

OTABENGA: Houses taller than trees. Villages that go on for days. Maybe these are great lies. Maybe not... Now begins my greatest hunt. To test my spirit against the

white world. To know their secrets. To become so like
my prey that I am invisible... Hunting the Land of the
Dead.

END OF ACT TWO

ACT THREE

Scene One

(The Saint Louis World's Fair of 1904. A snappy, Sousa-like march plays cheerfully in the background as bold bunting drops from the flies. Mid-stage, a BARKER *barks. A* TUBA PLAYER, *in full dress, provides the appropriate oom-pah-pah accompaniment)*

BARKER: "Of the primitive peoples brought from the four corners of this great planet to be exhibited at this great fair in the fourth year of the new century, none, not one, draws such enormous crowds of thrill-seekers day and night as the savage man-eater from deepest, darkest Africa, the authentic pygmy cannibal...Otto Bingo!"

(Cymbals crash, the tuba plays. Oom-pah-pah, etc)

(A couple enters, wanders downstage and faces the audience: a FAIRGOER 1, *with cigar, camera, newspaper and wife,* FAIRGOER 2. *They are well dressed and dignified. This, after all, is a scientific exhibition)*

BARKER: "What does this tiny savage think? What does he feel? And—here's the scary part, at least for this observer—what will he eat? Scientists from around the globe have gathered here in Saint Louis, Missouri to solve the mystery of the pygmy cannibal."

(Oom-pah-pah, etc. The music stops abruptly. The BARKER *and his* TUBA PLAYER *stand by, somewhat idly, in case they*

are needed. They exhibit signs of boredom: they've gone through this routine a hundred times. The two FAIRGOERS *peer into the distance.)*

FAIRGOER 1: This is the pygmy habitat? I don't see anything.

FAIRGOER 2: They are extremely tiny.

FAIRGOER 1: I can't perform an observation if there is nothing to observe.

FAIRGOER 2: Look! Lloyd. There's one.

FAIRGOER 1: Where?

FAIRGOER 2: Look!

FAIRGOER 1: Where?

FAIRGOER 2: Just to the left of the German beer garden. No, he's gone.

(A beat. A sense of disappointment)

FAIRGOER 1: *(To the* BARKER*)* I say. My good man.

(The BARKER *and the* TUBA PLAYER *snap to it, ready for duty.)*

FAIRGOER 1: Will we be able to observe the pygmy at closer quarters?

BARKER: *(His official speech)* "The specimen is believed to be twenty-three years of age. He will never grow larger than a well-fed, ten-year-old boy."

(That's the TUBA PLAYER's *cue: Oom-pah-pah, etc. The* BARKER *cuts him off.)*

FAIRGOER 1: Yes, but will the pygmy approach us?

BARKER: "Jungle life is fraught with danger. The *Saint Louis Post-Dispatch* reports that the pygmy's late wife became a neighboring tribe's main course for dinner."

(TUBA PLAYER's *cue: Oom-pah-pah, etc;* BARKER *cuts him off.)*

FAIRGOER 2: Lloyd! Look!

FAIRGOER 1: Where?

FAIRGOER 2: Look!

FAIRGOER 1: Where!?

FAIRGOER 2: *(Pointing up)* The orange dirigible... Come down...down... There!

FAIRGOER 1: Where?

FAIRGOER 2: Oh, he's gone.

(Suppressing his exasperation, FAIRGOER 1 *turns to the* BARKER, *but before he can speak.)*

BARKER: "Science has discovered a great deal about the cannibal pygmy race. If captured young and given the right diet, they make excellent servants."

(Oom-pah—and he's cut off.)

FAIRGOER 1: But will I actually *see* one?

FAIRGOER 2: There! He's right over there! Oh...

BARKER: "They have no religion, no traditions, no knowledge of handicraft or agriculture. They are cunning and devious, and enjoy torturing animals."

(Oom-pah-pah, and cut)

FAIRGOER 1: *(To his wife)* I am headed for the sliding elephant.

FAIRGOER 2: Lloyd.

FAIRGOER 1: At least you can *see* the elephant.

BARKER: "Pygmies have a snout-like jaw, similar to the common groundhog. Their skin is entirely covered by a thick pelt or fur."

(The BARKER *gives the "cut" sign to the* TUBA PLAYER *before he can get in his "Oom-pah-pah".)*

FAIRGOER 1: Why doesn't he just emerge?

FAIRGOER 2: This is how he behaves in his native habitat.

FAIRGOER 1: Damned rude.

FAIRGOER 2: There! No...

(Oom-pah-pah, unsolicited, from the TUBA PLAYER. *The* BARKER *cuts him off again.)*

FAIRGOER 1: The elephant slides at two.

FAIRGOER 2: Lloyd.

FAIRGOER 1: I don't intend to miss it.

FAIRGOER 2: We are here for scientific edification.

FAIRGOER 1: The Eskimos were edifying. They stood in plain sight.

FAIRGOER 2: We can see the elephant tonight.

FAIRGOER 1: *(Amazed)* He slides at *night*?

BARKER: "No pygmy has ever before stepped foot in the Western hemisphere. They express no regrets at their cannibalism. Their brains are forty cubic inches smaller than the Caucasian. Their women have been described as pretty little nut-brown maids."

FAIRGOER 1: *(To the* BARKER) Look, would you shut up!?

(A beat. Silence. The BARKER *and the* TUBA PLAYER *exchange glances. Wearing a hurt look, the* BARKER *approaches.)*

BARKER: It's the tuba, isn't it?

FAIRGOER 1: I am trying to sight a pygmy.

BARKER: I've tried everything.

FAIRGOER 1: Do you mind?

BARKER: He couldn't carry a tune if I strapped one on his back.

FAIRGOER 2: There he is!

(The two FAIRGOERS *peer into the distance)*

BARKER: I had a class act once. I was at Coney Island.

FAIRGOER 2: I think he went into that shack.

FAIRGOER 1: What shack?

BARKER: *(To the* TUBA PLAYER*)* You couldn't have got into Coney Island with a gun.

FAIRGOER 1: That's a hut, not a shack.

BARKER: *(Resigned to his fate)* Come on, let's go. It's time for the hairy Ainu.

(As the BARKER *prepares to leave, the* TUBA PLAYER *gestures to him.)*

BARKER: What? What is it?

*(*TUBA PLAYER *whispers in his ear.)*

BARKER: We've seen the sliding elephant four times already. *(A look from the* TUBA PLAYER*)* Oh, all right.

(The BARKER *exits, accompanied by the* TUBA PLAYER, *who puts his hand upon his boss's shoulder, attempting to console him.)*

BARKER: At Coney Island, we had classical tubists. They could do *Flight of the Bumble Bee.*

(They're gone. The FAIRGOERS *have continued dutifully to stare into the distance, trying to sight the pygmy...)*

*(*OTABENGA *wanders on, upstage, unseen. He is dressed in a ludicrous "primitive" costume, something out of a sideshow. With curiosity, he observes this strange couple.)*

FAIRGOER 2: Throw a stone.

FAIRGOER 1: Why?

FAIRGOER 2: See if he emerges.

(FAIRGOER 1 *begins to search the ground for a stone*)

FAIRGOER 1: A stone... (FAIRGOER 1 *discovers the feet of* OTABENGA. *Shtick: a slow look up, then back down, then he slinks back toward his wife*) Doris.

FAIRGOER 2: I think I see him.

FAIRGOER 1: So do I.

(FAIRGOER 1 *tugs at his wife's sleeve.* FAIRGOER 2 *turns, sees* OTABENGA, *returns, eyes front and wide.*)

FAIRGOER 2: Lloyd.

FAIRGOER 1: He's out of his habitat.

FAIRGOER 2: He escaped. What do we do?

FAIRGOER 1: Don't show fear. Just slowly... Back away...

(*They slowly back away.*)

OTABENGA: (*Offering his hand*) How do you do!

FAIRGOER 1: Oh God.

FAIRGOER 2: He wants to shake your hand.

OTABENGA: (*To the woman*) How do you do!

FAIRGOER 1: He wants to shake *your* hand.

FAIRGOER 2: I'm a woman.

(OTABENGA *lightly taps the woman's arm and insists on a handshake.*)

OTABENGA: How do you do!

FAIRGOER 2: Lloyd, he struck me.

FAIRGOER 1: I saw it.

FAIRGOER 2: I've been struck by a pygmy.

OTABENGA: How do you do?

FAIRGOER 1: This will not go unanswered.... Ready?

FAIRGOER 2: Yes.

FAIRGOER 1: Run for it!

(Exit, running for it, the two FAIRGOERS. *A beat, and enter* VERNER.*)*

VERNER: Otabenga how?

OTABENGA: I gave them your greeting. Why are they afraid? The other ones are wild. They throw things and shout. I want my arrows back.

VERNER: No! Chief McGee say, no more arrow. Too close. Lady from Cleveland. Ruin hat.

OTABENGA: A very ugly hat. I'm cold, Fwela. At night, and in the mornings.

VERNER: Blanket. Fwela bring.

OTABENGA: I want clothes like yours.

VERNER: No, Ota.

OTABENGA: And shoes. All the dead wear shoes.

VERNER: Native costume, must wear.

OTABENGA: I'm dressed like a banana tree!

VERNER: Fwela must go.

OTABENGA: I go with you.

VERNER: Otabenga stay.

OTABENGA: Am I a prisoner?

VERNER: America custom. People come, see you.

OTABENGA: I can't be chained to one spot. I can't sleep in there, I can't eat. *(Fingering the talisman hanging from* VERNER*'s neck)* I should have kept this for myself.

(Exit OTABENGA. *The lights rise on Chief* MCGEE*'s office)*

MCGEE: He's not cooperating, Reverend.

(VERNER *reluctantly joins his employer.*)

MISS FAIRCHILD: The Patagonians cooperate.

MCGEE: So do the Eskimos.

MISS FAIRCHILD: The hairy Ainu are probably the most polite primitive people you'll ever meet. The way they bow?

MCGEE: But your pygmy seems to enjoy causing trouble. Why is that, Reverend?

VERNER: Well, from the sociological point of view—

MCGEE: Sneaking up on the fairgoers.

VERNER: They provoked him.

MCGEE: Why do you always take the pygmy's side, Reverend?

VERNER: I want him let out.

MISS FAIRCHILD: Impossible.

MCGEE: Why?

VERNER: He's a hunter. He's not used to being confined.

MCGEE: I don't see any of the other specimens "walking around".

MISS FAIRCHILD: The Apaches are hunters, too.

MCGEE: They don't go "walking around". You're very close to your specimen, Reverend.

MISS FAIRCHILD: In more ways than you think.

MCGEE: I am under enormous pressure. This race theory business is a minefield, let me tell you. I am being attacked as a radical!

MISS FAIRCHILD: Face it, you made a stupid mistake.

MCGEE: I merely theorized that blood mixture would one day lead to a single, superior human race.

MISS FAIRCHILD: Racial interbreeding? You call that smart?

MCGEE: I meant interbreeding of the *white* races! Italians and, and, I don't know, the Dutch.

MISS FAIRCHILD: Anarchists in wooden shoes. That's improvement?

MCGEE: How could they misconstrue that? I stated publicly that the inferior races, quote, may not be trusted on horseback but only in the rear of the wagon. And now I'm some sort of radical integrationist who wants to load up the wagon with Hottentots!

MISS FAIRCHILD: Clumsy language. It's your own fault.

MCGEE: I am one of America's preeminent anthropologists!

VERNER: Excuse me, but I was hoping to discuss my position with the Anthropology Department.

MCGEE: We're overstaffed as it is.

VERNER: My personal funds—I've had enormous expenses—

MISS FAIRCHILD: The Palace of Electricity is looking for a door guard.

VERNER: I am a scientist, dammit!

MCGEE: There's no need for language, Reverend.

VERNER: I need a job!

MCGEE: *(To* MISS FAIRCHILD*)* He could help out with Anthropology Days.

MISS FAIRCHILD: We have everyone we need.

MCGEE: How are you at scientific calibration, Reverend? Anthropometrics?

VERNER: Anthropo—?

MCGEE: "Metrics."

VERNER: Second nature. I can do it in my sleep.

MCGEE: We'll be conducting some experiments. You could help out. Do a little lecturing.

MISS FAIRCHILD: And keep an eye on your pygmy.

MCGEE: Good point. How's five dollars sound?

VERNER: I risked my life—! I have a university degree—!

MCGEE: Six dollars. We expect exemplary behavior from the specimens.

(Lights fade in the office as MCGEE. MISS FAIRCHILD and VERNER exit. Lights up low on OTABENGA, opposite)

OTABENGA: "So tiny!" "But frightening." "Get him to smile, Harold. So we can see his teeth." "He is one of God's creatures. He deserves our prayers." "Toss him this hot dog. See if he goes for it." "What an ugly little bastard." "Dance, Pygmy. Here's a penny. Dance, Pygmy."

Scene Two

(Sounds of a city street. Enter VERNER, with a coat and hat for OTABENGA. Throughout, VERNER is nervous. He is taking a risk)

VERNER: Here, put these on. Hurry up. Stay by my side. Don't get lost in this crowd. We have to be back before Chief McGee finds out you're missing.

(OTABENGA dresses in the coat and hat)

VERNER: Look, Otabenga: the power and promise of a great city. Buildings that reach to the sky, built of stone to last for centuries. Automobiles, look! The combustion engine. Nothing like this in the forest!

OTABENGA: What is the death in it?

VERNER: Death?

OTABENGA: Yes, since it exists here. And you, Fwela: how long have you been dead?

VERNER: I'm not dead.

OTABENGA: Once long ago, before you lost your color, you were alive.

VERNER: My color?

OTABENGA: Once, Fwela, you were black as me.

VERNER: I was?

OTABENGA: All of you were. But don't despair. Your color is still inside you, somewhere. *(Sounds of a department store)* What is this place, Fwela?

(Shoppers, dressed fashionably, begin to cross. The first to do so wheels a display table of women's apparel, and places it; the second person to cross wheels a female mannequin, and places that.)

VERNER: "Department store." Everything you need, under one roof. Kitchen appliances, furniture, toiletries.

(OTABENGA picks up a woman's hat decorated with artificial fruit.)

OTABENGA: Things like this, Fwela?

VERNER: Put that back.

OTABENGA: Is this for eating?

VERNER: No, that's for wearing.

(OTABENGA puts it on.)

VERNER: *(Snatching the hat)* Not you.

(OTABENGA picks up another hat and puts it on VERNER's head.)

VERNER: *(Snatching the hat off)* Not for me, either.

(Business: OTABENGA *grabs another hat, tries it on;* VERNER *immediately snatches it off, places it back on the table. Again, etc.)*

VERNER: Will you stop? This is an American department store.

*(*OTABENGA *turns to the mannequin. Business: he handles her, looks under her skirt, etc)*

OTABENGA: Fwela, look. She is even more dead than you.

VERNER: Behave yourself.

*(*OTABENGA *has picked another clothing item from the table: a bra)*

OTABENGA: Ah. A weapon.

(He tries it like a slingshot; VERNER *tries to grab it away,* OTABENGA *grabs it back, etc. A* SHOPPER *crosses, an elegantly dressed woman. The two men try to cover. She slows, eyes* VERNER *and* OTABENGA *suspiciously, these two bizarre characters fighting over a bra, then exits)*

VERNER: *(Grabbing the bra)* Let me see that. A weapon? *(He tries it as a slingshot)* Takaa!

*(*OTABENGA, *using another bra, does the same.)*

(Enter a FLOOR WALKER, *unseen at first by the two delinquents)*

FLOOR WALKER: I beg your pardon.

*(*VERNER *and* OTABENGA *freeze, then guiltily replace the items. While the* FLOOR WALKER *addresses* VERNER, OTABENGA *takes a position behind the* FLOOR WALKER *and does some business: mimics the* FLOOR WALKER, *tries on another hat, etc.)*

FLOOR WALKER: This is Women's Apparel. There are no Negroes allowed in Women's Apparel. Or elsewhere. Ever.

(The FLOOR WALKER *checks behind him;* OTABENGA *covers, smiles sweetly.)*

VERNER: Sir, this man is an honored guest of the United States of America.

FLOOR WALKER: Perhaps. But not in Women's Apparel.

(Business: FLOOR WALKER *turns, catches* OTABENGA *in the act.)*

FLOOR WALKER: Get out of here immediately! Both of you!

*(*VERNER *and* OTABENGA *scamper out of the store laughing, and come to a rest, as the* FLOOR WALKER *exits. A beat)*

VERNER: I kept my promise. I got you out to see the city.

OTABENGA: You are good to me, Fwela.

(The sound of polite applause. MISS FAIRCHILD *appears, wearing a lab coat and armed with a pointer.* VERNER *gently removes* OTABENGA's *hat.)*

VERNER: I meant to tell you. A meeting. I promised Chief McGee you'd be there. No one will hurt you.

*(*MISS FAIRCHILD, *presiding, speaks to the assembled scientists.)*

MISS FAIRCHILD: Gentlemen, the tiny pygmy specimen. We begin with the science of craniometry. What connection has skull size to intelligence? Professor Verner.

*(*VERNER *reads the tape measurement he has just taken of* OTABENGA's *head.)*

VERNER: Twenty-seven and a quarter.

MISS FAIRCHILD: Adequate even for a white male. Professor?

(VERNER *measures his own head in the same fashion.*)

VERNER: Twenty-six and a half.

MISS FAIRCHILD: Ergo, gentlemen: Size has *no* connection to intelligence.

(*Polite applause as* VERNER *measures* OTABENGA*'s arm*)

VERNER: Thirty-three and a half.

MISS FAIRCHILD: Note, however, the extraordinary length of the arm.

VERNER: It's standard length. I wear a thirty-three and a half.

MISS FAIRCHILD: (*Ignoring him*) The dynamometer rating, Professor.

VERNER: Caucasian male: 40.5. African Pygmy: 55.6.

MISS FAIRCHILD: Their brute power, gentlemen. Professor?

VERNER: Umbilical-penile gap.

MISS FAIRCHILD: Abdominal elongation, the distance between the navel and the base of the penis. I see some of you whispering, gentlemen. Please bear in mind that I am a woman of the twentieth century.

VERNER: Caucasian male: 13 inches. African pygmy: 8.5.

MISS FAIRCHILD: The approximate gap in a ten year-old white boy. Mandibular projection?

VERNER: Pronounced.

MISS FAIRCHILD: The large jaw, gentlemen: the effect of a "fleshy" diet?

(*Light laughter, applause*)

VERNER: Distended nasal cartilage.

MISS FAIRCHILD: Olfactory defense.

VERNER: Acute enopthalmosis.

MISS FAIRCHILD: The deep-set eyes. We draw no conclusions, gentlemen. We limit ourselves to empirical observation. Next on the program, Professor?

VERNER: Verbal skills.

MISS FAIRCHILD: You'll enjoy this, Gentlemen. Professor Verner has attempted to teach the specimen some English.

VERNER: Thank you. As you know, gentlemen, on my many sojourns across the Dark Continent—

MISS FAIRCHILD: Professor.

VERNER: Yes. Good morning, Otabenga. *(A beat. Silence)* He's really quite intelligent—

OTABENGA: Horse shit.

VERNER: He's picked up some language from the fairgoers—

OTABENGA: Ugly little bastard. Throw a rock, see if he emerges.

MISS FAIRCHILD: That's enough, Professor. Next, the question of inherent violence in the cannibal species. Let us observe. Professor.

(VERNER hands OTABENGA a doll.)

OTABENGA: Fwela, what am I supposed to do with this?

MISS FAIRCHILD: Gentlemen, the specimen has spoken in his native tongue. Professor, you may converse with him.

VERNER: Stay, Otabenga. Almost over.

OTABENGA: How much longer do I stand here in a room full of cannibals?

VERNER: *(To the assembly)* He says that he finds the doll, uh, cute.

*(*OTABENGA *hurls the doll to the floor.)*

MISS FAIRCHILD: There you have it, Gentlemen. And now: resistance to pain. The hat pin.

VERNER: The hat pin!?

MISS FAIRCHILD: Stand back, Professor.

VERNER: No!

MISS FAIRCHILD: We're not going to harm him.

VERNER: Stay away!

MISS FAIRCHILD: You're interfering with a scientific experiment.

VERNER: *(To the assembled scientists)* He's just as intelligent as any of you, in his own way! We could learn from him—!

(Light laughter, applause)

MISS FAIRCHILD: That's enough, Professor.

VERNER: Leave us alone!

*(*VERNER *whisks* OTABENGA *off stage.)*

MISS FAIRCHILD: Gentlemen, we'll take a brief intermission and return with the Zulu tribesman. Thank you.

*(*MISS FAIRCHILD *exits, in pursuit. Lights down. Music)*

Scene Four

*(Night. The sound of pygmy singing, low and distant.
OTABENGA, alone in his habitat at the Fair)*

OTABENGA: I hear your song tonight. So far away...
This must be where they all come, even the ones killed
in the forest. A stream of spirits moving across the
ocean, trailing their color, staining the waters... Here,
they put the living behind fences and laugh at us. Even
if I could sing you this story, you would not believe it...

(A BAMBUTI WOMAN appears.)

BAMBUTI WOMAN: No man can sing your story,
Otabenga.

OTABENGA: You're here! I knew I could find you! We'll
be together again!

*(OTABENGA reaches unsuccessfully for BAMBUTI WOMAN;
she remains beyond his grasp.)*

OTABENGA: We'll be together again!

BAMBUTI WOMAN: Picture the forest, Otabenga. All that
you have given up forever.

OTABENGA: No. I'll take you back.

BAMBUTI WOMAN: There is no way back.

OTABENGA: I can do it. I'm alive. And I'm a hunter,
maybe the greatest hunter.

BAMBUTI WOMAN: Do you remember that last night?

OTABENGA: I didn't know.

BAMBUTI WOMAN: You knew. You left us.

OTABENGA: The hunt. I had to go.

BAMBUTI WOMAN: When the soldiers came for us,
I cried out for you.

OTABENGA: How could I have known?

BAMBUTI WOMAN: My last word was your name.
Poor Otabenga. See how far your hunt has brought
you this time. *(She turns to go.)*

OTABENGA: Don't go!

BAMBUTI WOMAN: To become so like your prey, your
true self is invisible. There is only one way to be like
the Dead.

*(*BAMBUTI WOMAN *is gone. Distant sounds of band music,
laughter, fireworks)*

(Enter VERNER *as lights rise. The sounds of a band playing
something Sousa-esque)*

VERNER: It's ending, Otabenga. The Fair is over.
You can go home now.... What's wrong? You're crying.
(He turns to address the gathering crowd) Ladies and
gentlemen! The genuine pygmy cannibal from the
African Congo! He dances to the dark spirit world
of the jungle forest. He dances in thanks to the people
of America. Is he so different, ladies and gentlemen,
from you or me? With proper training he could learn
to live among us. He loves music and song. He loves
this great country. He loves you, ladies and gentlemen.
I give you...Otabenga!

(Music plays. The lights begin to fade)

END OF ACT THREE

ACT FOUR

Scene One

*(The Belgian Congo, 1905. Pygmy encampment.
OTABENGA, downstage, speaks to the audience.
He is dressed in Western clothes identical to VERNER's.
Behind him is a large piece of cloth hanging from a crude
wooden frame, like a small theater curtain.)*

OTABENGA: You don't believe any of this, do you? You
think it's all a lie. No, no, don't deny it. But it's all true...
We shouldn't judge too quickly. I studied them closely.
The Dead are capable of goodness. No, I truly believe
that! They can be improved. Let me show you how it
was. Fwela will be me. We will be *muzungu.*

*(OTABENGA lifts the curtain to reveal VERNER seated in
a chair, his legs crossed, reading a book and smoking a pipe,
and sipping occasionally from a bowl. He places the needle
on the Edison phonograph next to him and a scratchy piece
of period American music is heard in the forest clearing)*

OTABENGA: *(To his audience)* "Observation" they call it.
We were displayed, like this. But we were prisoners.
Do you see? ...No, don't go. Stay, my friends. Please.

*(OTABENGA reluctantly lowers the curtain on VERNER.
Enter MASISI.)*

MASISI: You can't blame them.

OTABENGA: You believe me, Masisi.

MASISI: I see you came back. And you're not white—
on the outside.

OTABENGA: So many things I don't understand yet.
This is the greatest hunt of my life.

MASISI: And maybe the last. I am your friend,
Otabenga. I want you to remember that. I never wished
you any harm. So you should never wish me any harm.
Or cast any spells on me.

OTABENGA: Masisi.

MASISI: Or on my family.

OTABENGA: You know me—

MASISI: I do, I'm your friend, that's why they picked
me to tell you.

OTABENGA: Tell me what?

MASISI: Go away.

OTABENGA: What?

MASISI: Another part of the forest, the Land of the
Dead, anywhere. You are banished.

OTABENGA: Why?

MASISI: The dead is in you now. This one has your soul.
(He lifts the curtain again to reveal VERNER *seated in the
same manner as before.)* Go. And take that with you. *(Exit)*

VERNER: Can I tell you something, Otabenga? I love it
here. I'm at peace. At home, I never fit in. I need to be
free to dream. In America, you have to keep up with
the doers, the money-makers. But here... The forest
is where dreams were born. *(The bowl he's been sipping
from.)* What is this?

OTABENGA: Palm wine.

VERNER: I don't have to want here. I am honored and
looked up to. Here I am Fwela. You made me that. And

I love you for it. I, Samuel Phillips Verner, grandson of a Confederate officer—I am saying "I love you" to an African pygmy! I am free of myself! How can I ever repay you?

OTABENGA: Take me back.

VERNER: Back. Leave here?

OTABENGA: Now, Fwela.

VERNER: You don't know what you're saying. I can show you how to turn this wine into liquor. And cotton will grow here, I know it will.

OTABENGA: The forest is gone now. We're going back. *(He exits.)*

VERNER: Back to America? No, that's madness. They'll grind your bones into dust and scatter you to the winds. *(Calling after him)* Your own gods will never forgive you. I won't do it! I won't go back!

(The sound of a train whistle. Lights, music. Transition. OTABENGA *returns, dressed in the same suit as* VERNER.)

Scene Two

(Autumn, 1906. VERNER *and* OTABENGA *on a train headed for New York.* VERNER *brandishes a pocket flask.)*

VERNER: He laughed at me. Laughed in my face. "Have you tried the circus, Reverend?" The bastard. After everything I did for his god damn Fair... Saint Louis is out. I telegraphed the Smithsonian. No reply. In Dayton, they wouldn't even talk to me.

OTABENGA: I love trains, Fwela.

VERNER: They treat me like a traveling salesman.

OTABENGA: All the noise and steam.

VERNER: I am a scientist!

OTABENGA: Just to go from one place to another.

VERNER: "The Anthropology Department has all the
African specialists we need. All the Africans, too."
I could see the smirk on his face. *(He takes a drink.)*

OTABENGA: Fwela.

(OTABENGA gestures that he would like a sip from
VERNER's *flask.)*

VERNER: Do you know what it's like to be without
money in this country?

OTABENGA: Fwela?

VERNER: You're like a stray dog.

OTABENGA: Fwela?

VERNER: Table scraps. Bones.

OTABENGA: I'll have a taste of that, Fwela.

VERNER: Pygmies don't drink Kentucky bourbon.
(The flask is empty.) God damn it. This is cursed,
the whole idea.

OTABENGA: All will be well, Fwela.

VERNER: I've got important responsibilities.

OTABENGA: As long as we stay together.

VERNER: I can't be dragging a pygmy all over New
York City.

OTABENGA: We're a part of each other now. *(Tenderly he
feels* VERNER's *forehead.)* Fever again, Fwela. What am I
going to do with you?

VERNER: Don't talk pygmy here, I told you. It makes
people nervous. And get back in Third Class before the
porter shows up.

OTABENGA: Put your head back. Try to rest.

VERNER: I don't need to rest!

OTABENGA: Fwela?

VERNER: What?

OTABENGA: For the wintertime, we'll both need long, heavy coats.

VERNER: You are the most stubborn little...

OTABENGA: And hats.

VERNER: Now you listen to me. I've got one last card to play. I've written to William Temple Hornaday. He runs a kind of museum.

OTABENGA: What is museum?

VERNER: Well, it's where they show old, valuable things. He might want to show you.

OTABENGA: I am not old.

VERNER: It's not a museum, exactly. It's called the Bronx Zoological Society.

OTABENGA: I don't understand.

VERNER: Where they keep animals.

OTABENGA: You wouldn't put me with animals, Fwela.

VERNER: It would only be temporary. It would bring us in some money. (A beat) Don't look at me like that. You have to pull your own weight. That's an American principle.

OTABENGA: Four days and four nights I sat by your side. You were on fire.

VERNER: I paid my debt to you—

OTABENGA: I bathed you. I fed you.

VERNER: I bought you that suit with my own money!

OTABENGA: We can't separate. It would not be right.

VERNER: You just don't understand! You can't dress up in a suit of clothes and walk into my world. There's a wall here, right here, between you and me.

OTABENGA: A wall here?

VERNER: A wall, dammit! A wall!

(OTABENGA *walks through the "wall".*)

OTABENGA: There is no wall.

VERNER: Don't you defy me!

(VERNER, *in anger, grabs* OTABENGA. *Enter a* PORTER)

PORTER: Hey, whoa, there, whoa!

(VERNER *releases* OTABENGA)

PORTER: Did this Negro strike you, sir? I can have him arrested, and put off at Dudleytown.

(OTABENGA *and* VERNER *stare at one another.*)

PORTER: Just say the word, sir, and we'll lock him up for assault.

VERNER: No. He's excitable, that's all.

PORTER: Tickets, please.

VERNER: Tickets? (*To* OTABENGA) Do you have the—? Where did I put—?

PORTER: Tickets, please.

VERNER: You, my friend, are standing inches away from the premier sensation of the Saint Louis World's Fair, and all you can say is, "Tickets, please"? This! is a genuine African pygmy cannibal. What do you say to that?

PORTER: I say we don't allow no cannibals in Second Class. Third Class neither.

VERNER: This ruthless little man-eater has teeth filed into razor sharp points, made for tearing human flesh.

PORTER: Go on.

VERNER: I can let you have a look...for a dollar.

PORTER: A dollar!

VERNER: They paid out two dollars in Saint Louis. But seeing as it's you... The sensation of the World's Fair, for fifty cents.

PORTER: I don't know. I might try it.

(PORTER *hands* VERNER *fifty cents.*)

VERNER: Otabenga: smile.

OTABENGA: I'm too sad.

PORTER: He's talking pygmy?

VERNER: Otabenga.

OTABENGA: When I get a promise, Fwela.

VERNER: Smile!

OTABENGA: No.

PORTER: I'll take back them fifty cents.

VERNER: Fwela find home.

PORTER: Now *you're* talking pygmy?

OTABENGA: Will you live there too?

VERNER: Fwela visit.

OTABENGA: Every day?

VERNER: Every day almost.

OTABENGA: Do you promise?

VERNER: Fwela promise.

(OTABENGA *smiles at the* PORTER)

PORTER: Good Lord Almighty.

(*Enter the* CHIEF PORTER, *and a* PASSENGER.)

PORTER: Hey, Chief, get a load of this. Pygmy cannibal.

CHIEF PORTER: In Second Class?

PORTER: Got sharp pointy teeth.

VERNER: The better to tear the flesh of his human victims, Gentlemen.

CHIEF PORTER: Not on this line, Mister. Got enough complaints as it is.

VERNER: This, sir, is the world-renowned Otabenga, late of the Saint Louis World's Fair.

PASSENGER: Hey, he was in the newspapers.

CHIEF PORTER: What's he doing all dressed up?

PORTER: You should see them teeth, Boss.

VERNER: I can offer a private viewing right here, on the spot, at the reduced rate of fifty cents.

PASSENGER: I'll have a go at that.

VERNER: Step right up. One man at a time.

PASSENGER: He don't bite, do he?

VERNER: Only when provoked. Smile, Otabenga.

PASSENGER: Holy shit.

CHIEF PORTER: Let me have a try at that.

PORTER: I might want another look.

PASSENGER: I got to tell the boys back in the dining car. *(He exits.)*

VERNER: Special half-price rates until four P M, gentlemen. Let us retire to the saloon car.

(They begin to exit)

VERNER: The man-eater's teeth. Sharp as a meat cleaver—and twice as deadly.

(They exit as the sounds of the train grow louder.)

Scene Three

(The office of WILLIAM TEMPLE HORNADAY, *director of the New York Zoological Society, popularly known as the Bronx Zoo.* HORNADAY *is conversing with* MADISON GRANT, *Zoo treasurer and self-styled essayist.* HORNADAY *reads from a manuscript)*

HORNADAY: "The mixture of two races will always give us a race reverting to the lower type... The cross between a white man and a Negro is a Negro. The cross between any of the three European races and a Jew is a Jew."

GRANT: Well?

HORNADAY: Hm. *(A beat)* "The melting pot must not be allowed to boil without control." You wrote this?

GRANT: I did.

HORNADAY: Title?

GRANT: *The Passing of the Great Race.*

HORNADAY: *The Passing...?*

GRANT: *Of the Great Race.*

*(*HORNADAY *tosses the manuscript on the desk)*

HORNADAY: It leaves you feeling...

GRANT: What?

HORNADAY: Informed. Damned informed.

GRANT: Biological incompatibility. It's scientifically documented. The African races are unable to adapt here.

HORNADAY: So that's where your repatriation proposal comes in. Send them back.

GRANT: Let's begin a national discussion. That's all
I am proposing.

HORNADAY: It's bold, Madison. Damned bold.

GRANT: There may be a few fireworks. But I'm a
spokesman now, William. Thrust into the role.

HORNADAY: You're the man for it. Cup of coffee?

GRANT: I don't take stimulants.

HORNADAY: Oh, neither do I. Wreaks havoc with
the circulation.

GRANT: William?

HORNADAY: Yes?

GRANT: What am I doing here? Attendance again?

HORNADAY: Madison, the numbers are disastrous.

GRANT: That's your problem, isn't it.

HORNADAY: I need your help.

GRANT: I'm not a magician.

HORNADAY: You're Zoo treasurer. You're influential.
You've hunted with Teddy Roosevelt, for God's sake.

GRANT: He never stopped talking all the way across
British East Africa. Lousy shot, too.

HORNADAY: Madison. The Board will listen to you.

GRANT: Get to the point, William.

HORNADAY: A pygmy.

GRANT: What?

HORNADAY: We need something that will draw crowds.

GRANT: This is a Zoological Society, not Coney Island.
We don't exhibit human beings.

HORNADAY: But that's just it. I've been in touch with this explorer person, a reverend. He is in possession of a genuine African pygmy.

GRANT: So?

HORNADAY: He's in trouble, financially.

GRANT: The pygmy?

HORNADAY: No, Reverend Verner. We could get an excellent price.

GRANT: Are you out of your mind, man? We can't be buying Negroes. This is the 20th century.

HORNADAY: I know that, Madison, of course. *(A beat)* We could lease him. We need to do something bold!

GRANT: Aren't pygmies cannibals?

HORNADAY: Yes! People will come in droves. We scatter a few large bones to heighten the effect. Is he man or beast? Or both? Decide for yourselves, Ladies and Gentlemen.

GRANT: It's madness.

HORNADAY: We'll make it scientific, play up the evolutionary angle. Madison, look: What is the one, essential thing that everyone in this country needs? Eh? Someone to be superior to! That's the American legacy! The pilgrims had the Indians, the Germans had the Irish, the Irish had the Italians. Now everyone can have a pygmy, do you see?

GRANT: Don't clutch at me, William.

HORNADAY: I need people at my zoo!

GRANT: But not in the cages, for God's sake. It's morally, ethically wrong.

HORNADAY: I know that. But from the *entertainment* angle? *(Going to the door)* You've got to meet him, Madison.

GRANT: Who?

HORNADAY: He's very clever. He's knows some English.

GRANT: William—

(HORNADAY *opens the door, and there stands* OTABENGA, *dressed in his ill-fitting suit.*)

HORNADAY: Well, come in, come in. Stand right here. Good. What do you think, Madison?

GRANT: Have you lost your senses?

HORNADAY: Why?

GRANT: No one will come to the zoo to see this.

HORNADAY: Picture him in a loin cloth. And I haven't shown you the best part. Come closer. Ota? Smile!

(OTABENGA *does so.*)

GRANT: Good God.

HORNADAY: You see? For tearing flesh.

OTABENGA: *(Extending his hand)* How do you do.

GRANT: *(Taken aback)* Did you teach him that?

HORNADAY: No, Verner did, I imagine.

OTABENGA: How do you do.

HORNADAY: He wants to shake your hand.

GRANT: William, really.

OTABENGA: Cigar? Got a light?

GRANT: I do not smoke.

OTABENGA: No Negroes in Women's Apparel.

GRANT: This is preposterous.

HORNADAY: That's enough, Otabenga.

OTABENGA: Pygmies don't drink Kentucky bourbon.

GRANT: *(Exiting)* I do not approve of this.

HORNADAY: My future could be on the line, Madison.

GRANT: I won't openly oppose you. That's the best I can promise.

OTABENGA: The hat pin, Gentlemen!

(Exit GRANT. HORNADAY *stands for a beat at the door, then indulges himself by making an unkind gesture toward the departed* GRANT. *He turns to face* OTABENGA, *who obediently makes the same gesture to* HORNADAY.)

HORNADAY: Don't do that. *(Crossing to him)* You don't fool me, you know. You understand a lot more than you let on. *(A beat)* We'll take this off. I want to see your musculature. *(He carefully removes* OTABENGA's *jacket)* We all play our roles, don't we? If you accept yours, you may profit from it. Shirt.

*(*OTABENGA *slowly unbuttons his shirt and removes it.)*

HORNADAY: So tiny. Remarkable.

OTABENGA: When I dress like you, you are frightened. Why is that?

HORNADAY: Your language: so musical.

OTABENGA: I know I cannot trust you.

*(*OTABENGA *hands his shirt to* HORNADAY.)*

HORNADAY: You can trust me, you know.

OTABENGA: But I can observe you and learn.

HORNADAY: We only want to observe you. You will come to no harm. I can promise that.

(A cage lowers on OTABENGA. HORNADAY *withdraws and exits.)*

(After a long beat, enter the REVEREND JAMES H GORDON, *leader of the Colored Baptist Ministers' Conference. He speaks to the public.)*

GORDON: I have been apprised, Ladies and Gentlemen, of a damnable act. And I am come to the New York Zoological Society to appeal to every Christian-minded man and woman, to condemn this outrage. This is an insult to every colored citizen of this city, to humankind itself! Two days running, in a cage with a monkey. A man, with a soul, displayed like a beast...

(HORNADAY *takes a similar, but more uncertain stance opposite and appeals to the same public.)*

HORNADAY: Really, there has been a great deal of sensational exaggeration...

GORDON: Bones, ladies and gentlemen, strewn about the cage. What are those meant to symbolize?

HORNADAY: A simple, educational exhibit...

GORDON: There are political motivations behind this act!

HORNADAY: Science is ever neutral.

GORDON: God will judge the men responsible.

HORNADAY: The Reverend Gordon's remarks, I mean, really. Deliberately inflaming racial tensions—

GORDON: Let it be known: I shall return here with a hundred demonstrators! We will not rest until this African is freed! *(Exit)*

HORNADAY: The highest attendance figures ever, in the history of the New York Zoological Society! We have struck a chord in the popular imagination. As to these charges of inhumane treatment, come see for yourselves. He's quite comfortable in the cage. And safe. After all, where else would he go? He wouldn't last a day on the streets of New York City.

(A reassuring smile, and exit HORNADAY, *awkwardly, hurriedly.)*

(Lights come up on OTABENGA, *pacing in his cage.)*

OTABENGA: The first thing to die is their hearts. That explains their loss of color... That first day, when they all crowded around the cage, reaching in at me and laughing, that's when I was afraid.

(Multiple arms, reaching into the cage from all sides. Noise of laughter, shouting)

OTABENGA: So many Dead! Five and six deep on all sides, the crowd. Their smell and noise. I prayed that the bars were strong enough to keep them out....

(Lights lower. Arms disappear. It is night. A beat, and VERNER *enters.)*

VERNER: Otabenga? ...I brought you a blanket, for sleeping.

OTABENGA: Get me out of here, Fwela.

VERNER: Soon.

OTABENGA: Not soon. Now.

VERNER: Keep your voice down, I'm not supposed to be here. A few more days.

OTABENGA: No few more days! Where is your promise to me?

VERNER: I'm sorry—

OTABENGA: *This* is the home you spoke of?

VERNER: Look, I had no choice—

OTABENGA: Now I understand why they come. I am alive. I am alive and they are afraid! And so are you!

VERNER: I warned you. You can't say I didn't.

(Enter GORDON. *He and* VERNER *look at one another a moment.* GORDON *slips* VERNER *a wad of bills.* VERNER *pockets them. With a last look at* OTABENGA, *he slinks away and exits.)*

GORDON: First Saint Louis, now New York. You have been used, my African friend. And others suffer for it. You have a lot to learn about this land. The Howard Colored Orphans' Asylum. I run it. You're a bit old to be an orphan, but we'll make an exception. Christian training, some language skills, and I will show them. I will show them the potential of the race. I will make you famous. But for the right reasons, this time. *(As he is leaving)* You are free, Otabenga. In a manner of speaking.

(Exit GORDON. *The cage rises from* OTABENGA. *After a beat, he follows and exits)*

(Lights down. Sounds of African music: male voices chanting, fast, furious, hauntingly beautiful. Then gradually these sounds are replaced by the notes of a piano, building as the lights rise slowly on the next scene)

END OF ACT FOUR

ACT FIVE

Scene One

(Lights are low, the atmosphere a bit odd, as befits the setting: OTABENGA's imagination. Enter three products of the time, or CITIZENS: a woman, CITIZEN 1, and two men, CITIZEN 2 and 3. Their manner of dress indicates membership in the leisure class. They have an expectant air about them.)

CITIZEN 1: We were wrong, of course.

CITIZEN 2: But attitudes change.

CITIZEN 1: It takes time.

CITIZEN 2: And good will.

CITIZEN 3: It's a bold move, you know.

CITIZEN 1: Inviting him to my home?

CITIZEN 2: It's wickedly progressive.

CITIZEN 3: He's famous now. That makes all of the difference.

CITIZEN 2: He's coming.

(Enter OTABENGA, in lab coat, with pointer.)

CITIZEN 1: *(Going to him)* Welcome, dear Sir!

CITIZEN 2: It is an honor, Sir.

OTABENGA: The honor is mine.

CITIZEN 3: You speak English like a native.

OTABENGA: I shall take that as a compliment.

CITIZEN 1: You will dine with us, of course.

OTABENGA: My pleasure, Madam.

CITIZEN 2: I understand you are a hunter, Mister Benga.

OTABENGA: Indeed, Sir.

CITIZEN 2: I go after duck, myself. I would be honored if you would be my guest.

CITIZEN 3: He will be boating this weekend, with me. That is, if you will accept my invitation, sir.

CITIZEN 1: You are becoming a celebrity in our city, Mister Benga.

CITIZEN 2: America loves a success story.

CITIZEN 3: We wish to hear more of your ideas.

CITIZEN 2: Your philosophy.

CITIZEN 3: Your insights.

OTABENGA: My message is this: do not lose hope. The Dead can be improved. *(Calling, off)* The specimen, please.

(Enter VERNER, *shirtless. He stands obediently at* OTABENGA's *side)*

OTABENGA: Let us remember, Gentlemen: Humility is a long hard road.

CITIZEN 1: Help us find our way, Otabenga!

OTABENGA: *(Using his pointer)* Observe, gentlemen, the absence of color. A sign of chronic morbidity?

VERNER: I am dead.

OTABENGA: Nasal projection.

VERNER: Pronounced.

OTABENGA: Their nosiness, Gentlemen. Their need to interfere. Body fur?

VERNER: Excessive.

OTABENGA: Their bear-like character. Reproductive organs?

VERNER: Protrusive.

OTABENGA: Their lecherous behavior. But what of their hearts, gentlemen?

CITIZEN 1: In our hearts—

CITIZEN 2: We mean to help.

OTABENGA: This urge to "help." How can they control it?

CITIZEN 3: Through training.

CITIZEN 2: Teach us! Please!

OTABENGA: Become the thing you are hunting, until your true self is invisible to it.

(In shadow, upstage, an INSTRUCTRESS has appeared. She is seated at the piano)

INSTRUCTRESS: Otabenga.

(When the CITIZENS and VERNER hear her voice, they freeze a beat, then exit quickly. OTABENGA turns to face the INSTRUCTRESS)

(When OTABENGA turns back, the others are gone. His reverie is over)

OTABENGA: Learn to live.

(The INSTRUCTRESS begins to play a few notes of the hymn Love Divine. *The lights come up. We are in a classroom at the Howard Colored Orphans Asylum. She continues to play softly as OTABENGA slowly removes his lab coat)*

INSTRUCTRESS: Your mind is wandering again. It gives an impression of laziness. Otabenga? *(Silence. She gets up, comes to him.)* You're going to be stubborn again today. Well, I will match you blow for blow, because I believe in you. Reverend Gordon believes in you. And we mean to help you. Bible training. Psalm 23. "The Lord is my shepherd." *(Silence. A beat)* Otabenga.

(Through the next few lines, OTABENGA begins to circle the INSTRUCTRESS, as if he is stalking her. His intent is sexual)

OTABENGA: "I shall not want."

INSTRUCTRESS: "He maketh me to lie down in green pastures." *(A beat)* "He leadeth..."

OTABENGA: "He leadeth me beside the still waters."

INSTRUCTRESS: "He restoreth my soul: he leadeth me in the paths of righteousness for his name's sake."

(OTABENGA reaches out for INSTRUCTRESS, tenderly; she rejects him firmly)

INSTRUCTRESS: No.

OTABENGA: "Yea, though I walk through the valley of the shadow of death, I will fear no evil."

(Again OTABENGA tries; again INSTRUCTRESS rejects him, more firmly this time.)

INSTRUCTRESS: I said no!

OTABENGA: "For thou art with me. Thy rod and thy staff, they comfort me."

(And again)

INSTRUCTRESS: You have been here ten months, you know the rules!

OTABENGA: "Love."

INSTRUCTRESS: "Love"? You don't understand the word. A dangerous word. "Apple." That's your word for today. (*She hands him a chalk slate.*) Write it for me. "A." (*A beat*) "A!"

(OTABENGA *drops the slate and grabs* INSTRUCTRESS'S *wrists*)

OTABENGA: If you knew how much I want you right now—

INSTRUCTRESS: English only!

OTABENGA: How I want to drag you outside, throw you on the ground—

INSTRUCTRESS: No native language in this room!

OTABENGA: And fuck you fuck you fuck you!

(*She frees herself*)

INSTRUCTRESS: Go stand in the corner! Right this instant!

(*Pause. They are both frozen in anger and defiance, glaring at one another*

(*Enter* GRANT *followed by* GORDON)

GRANT: How did you say our African is doing?

GORDON: He's making progress, Mister Grant.

GRANT: Toward what? Assault and battery?

INSTRUCTRESS: (*Moving to the piano*) Otabenga.

(INSTRUCTRESS *plays the hymn* Love Divine. *She has to coax* OTABENGA *with the first few words, but he soon overcomes his reluctance and takes over. His singing is strong and good and gains in power as the hymn progresses*)

INSTRUCTRESS:
Love divine, all loves excelling
Joy of heav'n, to earth come down.
Fix in us thy humble dwelling,
All thy faithful mercies crown.

Jesus, thou art all compassion,
Pure, unbounded love thou art;
Visit us with thy salvation,
Enter every trembling heart.
(She stops playing and stands.)

GRANT: Private singing lessons, Reverend?

GORDON: Tessie, this is Mister Madison Grant, the new member of our Board.

INSTRUCTRESS: *(Curtsying)* How do you do, sir?

GRANT: This is the sort of behavior that distresses the Board, Reverend.

GORDON: I don't follow you, sir.

GRANT: You don't follow me. Why do we fund the Howard Colored Orphans Asylum?

GORDON: Christian charity, sir.

GRANT: Yes, but we also want you to make something of the colored orphans. America does not need Negro opera singers, does it?

GORDON: Well, sir—

GRANT: Farm hands, carpenters, nannies, yes. The Board has ruled against any training in the arts.

GORDON: Oh, yes sir, I know.

GRANT: Then why, Reverend, behind our backs, do you teach them to read and write and sing?

GORDON: Me, sir?

GRANT: Reverend, really. We're not stupid.

GORDON: Yes, sir, and you're not blind and hateful either.

GRANT: I beg your pardon?

GORDON: And we need your money, sir, worse than I wish we did. So we always try, just as hard as we can, to do what you want. Even when it's wrong.

GRANT: We know what we're doing, Reverend.

GORDON: And I know what you're doing, too.

(*A beat.* GORDON *and* GRANT *stand closely, staring into one another's eyes*)

GRANT: (*Meaning the opposite*) I like you, Reverend.

GORDON: (*Meaning the opposite*) I like you, too, Mister Grant.

GRANT: You've got spirit.

GORDON: Sometimes that's all I'm allowed to have.

GRANT: It pains me to tell you this, but you will fail here.

GORDON: Will I?

GRANT: Trying to improve this African. Biological adaptability, Reverend. The race may not be up to it. That's not a criticism. I only mean to help.

GORDON: That is real white of you.

GRANT: This is pure science, nothing more. Research proves that segregation is in your own best interests.

GORDON: Is it?

GRANT: Race improvement, Reverend: You'll have to earn it, on your own, in your own society.

GORDON: Well. We all strive to improve, Mister Grant.

GRANT: But I hate to see you get your hopes up. Biological evolution is a slow process.

GORDON: Just how long do you estimate it will take us to evolve?

GRANT: Three or four centuries.

GORDON: I always figured we had a hard task, Mister Grant. But till I met you, I didn't realize what a back-breaker it is.

GRANT: Well, keep at it. And how is our African?

INSTRUCTRESS: He's doing wonderfully, Mister Grant.

GRANT: What trade is he learning?

(Too quickly:)

INSTRUCTRESS: Farming.

GORDON: Carpentry.

GRANT: Let's see what he can do. *(To* OTABENGA*)* Come here.

*(*OTABENGA *does so.)*

GRANT: How do you like the asylum?

(Silence. A beat)

INSTRUCTRESS: He's really quite shy.

GRANT: Speak up. You were quite a chatterbox the first time I met you. Do you miss the zoo? *(A beat)* Don't expect too much, Reverend. *(To* OTABENGA*)* If you don't know any words, can you make a sign? Hmm?

OTABENGA: How about this?

(A rude gesture from OTABENGA*)*

GRANT: *(To* GORDON*)* What is the meaning of this?

GORDON: *(Same gesture)* This, sir?

INSTRUCTRESS: He doesn't know what it means, Mister Grant.

GRANT: This will go on my report. *(As he exits)* I do not like what I see here. The blind teaching the blind.

(Exit GRANT. *A beat, and* GORDON *sends the* INSTRUCTRESS *out too)*

GORDON: You won't talk to me. But you understand everything I say. At night, you sneak through the halls, even though I expressly forbid it. What else do you do at night? *(Exploding)* She is fourteen years old! She's only a child herself! She was put in my care! This is how you repay me? *(A beat)* The only thing between you and prison is my reputation. I had a lot riding on you, Otabenga. All you had to do was fit in. Just fit in. I want you gone by dawn tomorrow. Gone: do you understand *that*?

(Exit GORDON. OTABENGA *remains a moment and observes as* VERNER *enters, then exits.)*

VERNER: *(To an imaginary audience)* Good evening, ladies and gentlemen, rubes and drunkards. My lecture tonight will be over your heads and too damn good for you. Let me begin with an observation: Not one of you is worthy to even kiss my ass...

(Richmond, Virginia, 1916. We are backstage at a lecture hall. VERNER *is dressed as the famous African explorer but he is a skid-row version now. He is drunk and trying to hide it.)*

(Enter a MANAGER, *stiffly dressed, harried and testy)*

MANAGER: Verner. Where in hell have you been? I warned you about being late again.

VERNER: I took a wrong turn.

MANAGER: The famous African explorer. Can't walk two blocks without getting lost.

VERNER: I will not be ridiculed by you, sir.

MANAGER: No, you do that just fine on your own. Pull yourself together. Do you even remember what town we're in? I'll give you a hint: Richmond, Virginia. Play up the cannibal bit, throw in some crocodiles. And I'm

warning you: you go all crazy on me again, you're
through. How drunk are you?

VERNER: I, sir? How is the crowd tonight?

MANAGER: "Crowd"? I sold more seats for the Siamese
twins from Baltimore.

VERNER: I was wondering if, for medicinal purposes,
you might advance me, say, six dollars.

MANAGER: Not a chance.

VERNER: Or five, then.

MANAGER: You're on, Reverend. *(Exit)*

VERNER: I may need to see a physician!

*(*VERNER *is caught in a bright spotlight just as he begins
to slip the flask from his pocket)*

VERNER: Good evening, ladies and gentlemen. My
lecture tonight is on the topic of the Dark Continent.
I explored there. I faced death there. I lived...with the
pygmies! The only white man ever to do so, ever...
Let me begin by offering an observation... *(A pause;
he has lost his train of thought)* The word "opportunity"
is the keynote to Africa today, my friends. What is
needed is not capital, no, but understanding and, uh—
(A beat, then snapping back to it) Africa, Ladies and
Gentlemen! Deadly poisonous snakes dropping from
the trees. Crocodiles the length of a modern motorcar.
Look! The pygmies! Tiny, savage man-eaters, they
rush their human victim, jab him with their spears,
the blood, the cries, into the giant pot with him, still
alive, ladies and gentlemen! Oh, the horror of it!
(A pause) And the lies. Stories told to fools like you
by liars like me. The Africa we invent so we can believe
in the America we've invented, too.

MANAGER: *(Off)* Verner!

VERNER: The Land of the Dead he called it here! The many ways of dying here, the ways we kill. We kill for difference. Into the giant melting pot until they're all boiled alike, then we swallow them up, cannibals... No bigger heart, ladies and gentlemen, no braver hunter, and I betrayed him, sold him, they displayed him in a cage! It's the deadness in me, that's why I did it, and it is in you too!

(VERNER's spotlight is cut. Silence... After a beat, enter the asylum NURSE from the first scene.)

NURSE: You're late for evening meal.

VERNER: I can't.

NURSE: Why not?

VERNER: The dining hall, it's full of madmen.

NURSE: Do you want me to withhold your medication?

VERNER: No!

NURSE: Then you have to come eat.

VERNER: I will, I just... Please?

NURSE: You need to finish the story again.

(She takes a chair, apart, furtively lights a cigarette and listens)

VERNER: It was 1916. An old couple approached me after the lecture. He was in Lynchburg, a few hours west.

(Enter OTABENGA. He wears the coveralls of a tobacco worker. The sounds of children laughing and taunting)

CHILDREN: *(Off-stage voices)* It's the pygmy! There goes the pygmy! Pygmy, pygmy! *(Etc)*

(As he moves, OTABENGA is halted by the children. He whirls, and tries to shoo them away; he ducks from something

they throw. Finally, with a fierce cry, he makes a run at them. The sounds stop abruptly.)

OTABENGA: The children are the only ones who notice anymore, Fwela. No one else speaks to me, or even looks me in the eye. Invisible at last.

VERNER: Aren't you glad to see me? Or surprised, at least?

(OTABENGA *stares at him a beat, expressionless.)*

OTABENGA: They give me work at the tobacco factory. Fifty cents a day and all I can smoke.

VERNER: You've had a hard time of it, I know. So have I. Damned malaria. They put me in a sanitarium. Lost track of you. I didn't mean for it to play out this way.... We never should have left the forest, Otabenga. That was our mistake. Let's go back. There's nothing for us here.

OTABENGA: The hunt is here.

VERNER: We catch a freighter at Norfolk, in a month we'll be back in the Congo.

OTABENGA: Together again? The two explorers?

VERNER: With the war in Europe, the price of cotton — we'll be rich in no time!

OTABENGA: "In no time"...I have thought a great deal about it, Fwela. The dead are a mysterious people. To understand them, to really know their secrets, you have to become them.

(OTABENGA *sits on the ground and tends a small fire.)*

VERNER: What is this place, Otabenga?

OTABENGA: This is where I come at night, to hear the singing. It is not much of a forest. But it is what I have.

(VERNER *sits next to* OTABENGA *at the fire.)*

VERNER: You'll be a legend now among your people.

OTABENGA: I lived with the dead. The only Bambuti ever to do so. I have the story. But no one to tell it to.

VERNER: You have me.

(OTABENGA *laughs softly, shakes his head.*)

VERNER: I'm worth something.

OTABENGA: I will say, Fwela, that you are surely the most alive dead person I know.

VERNER: Go back with me, Otabenga. Tell them the story.

(*The singing begins, softly at first, then rising: pygmy voices, hauntingly beautiful.*)

OTABENGA: The story is, the hunt ends here, with the hunter caught. To die in the Land of the Dead. It is all a great mystery. Or maybe a great joke, on me.

VERNER: I hear the singing.

OTABENGA: Dance, Fwela. To the forest inside you.

(*In the background,* VERNER *moves gracefully to the singing.*)

OTABENGA: Samuel Phillips Verner never returned to Africa. He never succeeded in growing cotton in the Congo. His book was never published. He spent time in an asylum, suffering from alcoholism and malaria. He died in 1943, at the age of seventy. (*He withdraws a gun from the pocket of his overalls.*) Otabenga, Bambuti hunter, settled in Lynchburg, Virginia, in the Land of the Dead. He never fit in. On the last night of winter, 1916, alone in the woods on the outskirts of town, he shot himself through the heart.

(*The singing stops.* VERNER *stops. The two men look at one another.* OTABENGA *has the gun pointed at his heart.*)

OTABENGA: Your last secret. I am you.

VERNER: No!

(*As* VERNER *takes a step toward* OTABENGA, *the lights go to black. A gunshot. Loud forest sounds... The sounds halt as the lights rise again on* VERNER, *by himself now... The* NURSE *rises and approaches.*)

NURSE: Always ends the same. No one there.

VERNER: He's there.

NURSE: A piece of advice, Reverend: If you want to get out of here anytime soon...he's not there.

VERNER: I betrayed him once. I won't do it again. Every leaf, every root. He's there. Always will be.

(*Exit* VERNER. *After a beat, the* NURSE *follows.*)

(*Lights. Music*)

END OF PLAY

CPSIA information can be obtained
at www.ICGtesting.com
Printed in the USA
LVOW03s1446140617
538110LV00010B/751/P

9 780881 454031